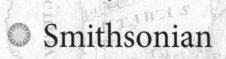

# Smithsonian

# Exploring
### the
# Delaware
## Colony

by Lori McManus

**CAPSTONE PRESS**
a capstone imprint

Smithsonian Books are published by Capstone Press,
1710 Roe Crest Drive, North Mankato, Minnesota 56003
www.capstonepub.com

**Library of Congress Cataloging-in-Publication Data**
Names: McManus, Lori, author.
Title: Exploring the Delaware Colony / by Lori McManus.
Description: North Mankato, Minnesota: Capstone Press, [2017] | Series:
  Smithsonian. Exploring the 13 Colonies | Includes bibliographical
  references and index. | Audience: Grades 4–6.
Identifiers: LCCN 2016002546| ISBN 9781515722397 (library binding) | ISBN
  9781515722526 (paperback) | ISBN 9781515722656 (ebook (PDF))
Subjects: LCSH: Delaware—History—Colonial period, ca. 1600–1775—Juvenile
  literature. | Delaware—History—1775–1865—Juvenile literature.
Classification: LCC F167 .M387 2017 | DDC 975.1/02—dc23
LC record available at http://lccn.loc.gov/2016002546

**Editorial Credits**
Gina Kammer, editor; Richard Parker, designer; Eric Gohl, media researcher;
Kathy McColley, production specialist

Our very special thanks to Stephen Binns at the Smithsonian Center for Learning and Digital Access for
his curatorial review. Capstone would also like to thank Kealy Gordon, Smithsonian Institution Product
Development Manager, and the following at Smithsonian Enterprises: Christopher A. Liedel, President;
Carol LeBlanc, Senior Vice President; Brigid Ferraro, Vice President; Ellen Nanney, Licensing Manager.

**Photo Credits**
Bridgeman Images: Courtesy of Historical Society of Pennsylvania Collection/Philadelphia History
Museum at the Atwater Kent, 21; Capstone: 4; Corbis: Bettmann, 9; Getty Images: MyLoupe, 10,
National Geographic/Stephen St. John, 30, Stock Montage, 25; Granger, NYC: 12, 20, 31; iStockphoto:
traveler1116, 26; Library of Congress: 24, 33, 41; Nativestock: Marilyn Angel Wynn, 13; New York
Public Library: 16; Newscom: Picture History, 36, Stock Connection Worldwide/Andre Jenny, 15, World
History Archive, 34; North Wind Picture Archives: cover, 7, 8, 11, 14, 18, 19, 22, 23, 27, 28, 29, 32, 35;
Shutterstock: rsooll, 37; SuperStock: 6; Wikimedia: Public Domain, 17, 39, 40

Design Elements: Shutterstock

# Table of Contents

# Introduction:
# The 13 Colonies

The United States started out as 13 **Colonies**. People moved to these colonies in the new land, but they were still subject to laws of their home countries. Their farms, buildings, trading posts, and other businesses in the new land were all part of what made up a colony.

Delaware was one of the smallest colonies, but three countries fought over its land.

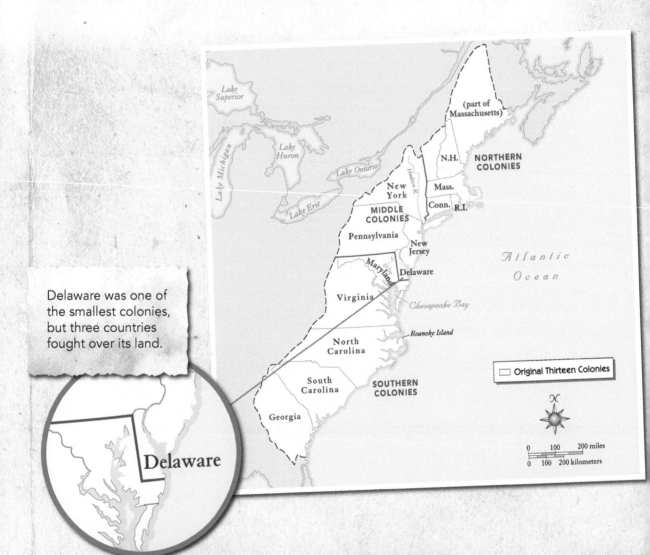

**colony**—a place that is settled by people from another country and is controlled by that country

# The Original 13 Colonies

The first permanent European settlement in each colony:

| | | | |
|---|---|---|---|
| Virginia | 1607 | **Delaware** | **1638** |
| Massachusetts | 1620 | Pennsylvania | 1643 |
| New Hampshire | 1623 | North Carolina | 1653 |
| New York | 1624 | New Jersey | 1660 |
| Connecticut | 1633 | South Carolina | 1670 |
| Maryland | 1634 | Georgia | 1733 |
| Rhode Island | 1636 | | |

The settlers of these colonies had many reasons for leaving their home countries. Some wanted the chance to own a farm. Some came to practice their religions freely. Other colonists were forced to leave home because they had committed crimes or owed the government money.

Virginia was the first English colony. In 1607 John Smith and about 100 English men and boys founded Jamestown in Virginia. This was the first permanent English settlement in North America. Georgia, the last of the original 13 Colonies, was settled in 1733.

Delaware, one of the smallest colonies, was ruled by three different European countries during its early years. The colony later earned the honor of becoming the first state in the United States. Like Delaware, each colony had a unique history. Yet all 13 faced struggles to survive and grow in a new land called America.

# Exploration of Delaware Bay

In the 1500s and 1600s, explorers and fur traders from Europe sailed to different parts of the world, including America. They sent reports back to Europe about what they found there. The nations of Europe then competed for control of lands and trading routes. If a nation controlled another land, it could grow rich from the **natural resources** and goods found there.

In the early 1600s, the Dutch government was seeking a shortcut to Asia. The Dutch, people of the Netherlands, hired an English sea captain named Henry Hudson to find this route. Hudson and his crew sailed across the Atlantic Ocean until they reached the eastern coast of Canada. Then they headed south. In August of 1609, Hudson sailed into what would be named Delaware Bay. He claimed the land for the Dutch, though Dutch settlers would not arrive there for another decade. Although Hudson did not go ashore, he reported to the Dutch East India Company, a trading company, what he saw. He claimed that the land of Delaware had "a white sandy shore, and within appeared a thick grove of trees full of green **foliage**."

This painting depicts Henry Hudson's exploration of Delaware Bay.

In 1610 an English sea captain named Samuel Argall sailed north from Virginia. He came upon the bay where Hudson had arrived. Argall named the bay after the governor of Virginia, Lord De La Warr. Argall claimed the land for England, but the English didn't immediately settle the area either. So Argall's claim wasn't worth much.

Lord De La Warr went to America to govern Virginia. Delaware was named in his honor.

## Did You Know?

North American colonists formed the name "Delaware" from "De La Warr." Delaware Bay, Delaware River, and the state of Delaware are all named after Lord De La Warr.

natural resource—a material found in nature that is useful to people
foliage—leaves

## New Lives

Settlers from Europe went to live in the American Colonies, including the Delaware Bay area. The new ways of life in the various colonies depended on the weather and the type of land in the region. In the Southern Colonies, the soil and mild climate allowed the colonists to grow crops that could be sold to Europe. They grew cotton, **indigo**, tobacco, and rice. In the Northern Colonies, most people kept small farms to grow food for their families. In the north it was too cold in the winter to depend on farming. The northern colonists created businesses based on fishing, shipbuilding, and trade. Delaware was one of the Middle Colonies. This region was perfect for growing grain, but other businesses also developed.

Settlers in the three Colonial regions all had to work hard to build their new lives.

*"... the Winter begins late in November ... and ends in the middle of January ... They know nothing of autumn and spring there, for when winter sets in, it sets in mighty suddenly ... Then it immediately becomes warm summer, with such a heat that the colonists who plant are not able to do anything in the middle of the day, during the summer."*

—Colonist Peter Lindstrom, 1654–1655

Delaware welcomed different religions in the colony.

## A Mixed Colony

Unlike most other colonies, Delaware was ruled by several different countries. Each group of people who settled there brought different culture and religion. Delaware practiced religious **tolerance** from its beginning. People of many religions were welcome in the colony. Delaware also welcomed **immigrants** from other colonies and countries, including German and Welsh settlers from Pennsylvania and Scots-Irish people from northern Ireland.

Many of Delaware's settlers were farmers and traders. Farmers sold their goods to traders. Traders then sold goods to Europe and to people in other colonies.

After the English took control, Delaware was never fully independent of the neighboring colony of Pennsylvania. But during the American Revolution, Delaware would have an important role to play in the independence of all the colonies.

**indigo**—a plant that produces a deep-blue dye

**tolerance**—the acceptance of people's beliefs or actions that differ from one's own beliefs or actions

**immigrant**—someone who comes from one coutnry to live permanently in another country

# Chapter 1:
# First People in Delaware

Long before the arrival of Europeans, the land now known as Delaware was home to Native Americans. The main tribe living in the area called themselves the Lenni Lenape, which means "original people."

The Lenni Lenape people lived in villages of hundreds of people along the Delaware River and nearby streams. Their homes, called **wigwams**, were round or long huts made of wood, bark, and grass. A hole at the top of each wigwam allowed the Lenni Lenapes to burn a fire inside for cooking and warmth. The smoke escaped through the hole.

Sometimes several Lenni Lenape families lived together in a larger wigwam called a longhouse.

## Daily Life

The Lenni Lenapes were mainly farmers. They grew corn, beans, squash, and sweet potatoes in the rich soil near the Delaware River. The women, older girls, and young children tended the crops. Women and their daughters also did the cooking. Corn was used in many dishes, including cornbread and succotash, which is a mixture of corn and beans.

Lenni Lenape men and their older sons fished and hunted. They caught fish using spears, wooden traps, hooks, and nets. They used bows and arrows to hunt geese, wild turkeys, bear, and deer. The meat was roasted and used for stews. Bones and antlers were shaped into farming tools, fishhooks, and arrowheads. Deerskins were made into clothing and shoes.

This woodcut shows a Lenni Lenape family with weapons and ceremonial clothing.

European David Zeisberger teaches his religion to the Lenni Lenapes in America.

## Values

The Lenni Lenapes were one of the most peaceful Native American tribes. They valued kindness to each other and to strangers. They enjoyed social events, games, and celebrations. Lenni Lenape chiefs helped to peacefully solve conflicts among villages and other tribes.

The Lenni Lenape people also had a strong belief in justice. Despite their peaceful nature, they declared war when necessary to protect themselves or to settle a wrong.

## Attitude toward the Land

The Lenni Lenapes moved to new areas each season. They made agreements with other tribes about the boundaries of their hunting grounds, fishing areas, and farmland. The Lenni Lenapes did not believe that people could own land permanently. Instead they believed that a tribe could use an area for a certain period of time. This attitude about the land would bring the Lenni Lenape people into conflict with the European settlers who arrived in the 1600s.

## Other Native Americans in Delaware

Other tribes lived in the Delaware Bay area before the arrival of the Europeans. The Nanticokes and Assateagues made their homes along the eastern banks of the Chesapeake Bay. Like the Lenni Lenapes, these Native Americans were farmers, hunters, and fishermen. The Nanticokes also made beautiful beads, which they used as money.

However, with the arrival of the Europeans, the number of Native Americans greatly declined. There may have been more than 20,000 Lenni Lenapes at the time the first Europeans came to America. But the Europeans brought new diseases such as **smallpox** and measles, which the native people couldn't fight off. Because of these diseases, along with wars between Native American tribes, many Lenni Lenapes died. There were only around 4,000 left by the 1680s.

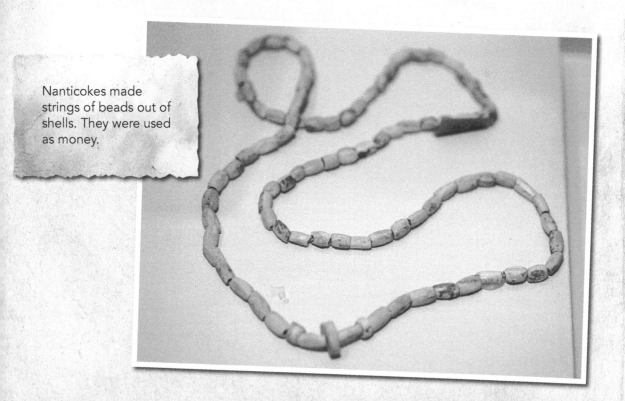

Nanticokes made strings of beads out of shells. They were used as money.

# Chapter 2:
# First Settlers: The Dutch

The Dutch were the first Europeans to explore and build homes in the area of Delaware. They wanted to settle the land that Hudson had claimed for them years earlier. This land included parts of present-day Delaware, New York, New Jersey, Pennsylvania, and Connecticut.

The Dutch were the first Europeans to arrive and settle in the Delaware area.

In 1629 the Dutch West India Company bought land near the entrance to the Delaware Bay from the Lenni Lenape chiefs. The trading company planned to set up a whaling, fishing, and fur-trading post. The location would make it easy for ships to come and go.

Soon a ship carrying 28 men arrived from the Netherlands. They called their settlement Zwaanendael, Dutch for "Valley of the Swans," because of the birds they saw on Delaware Bay. They built houses, a factory for removing oil from whale blubber, and a fort named Oplandt.

Delaware's Zwaanendael Museum is on the site of the first Dutch settlement.

## A Sad End

In 1632 merchant David Pietersen de Vries sailed to Zwaanendael with more Dutch settlers. When his ship arrived, the settlement was no longer there. The buildings were burned to the ground.

De Vries learned what happened from a Native American. Apparently the Dutch had hung up a tin sign that showed national symbols of the Netherlands. Not realizing the importance of the symbols, a Lenni Lenape chief took the sign and made tobacco pipes from the tin. The Dutch were furious!

David Pietersen de Vries sailed to America to bring more settlers to Zwaanendael. He found that the settlement was no longer there.

Dutch ships sail near Hoorn, the home of Captain de Vries in the Netherlands.

To calm the Dutch settlers, some of the Lenni Lenape people killed the chief who had taken the tin. This angered the chief's friends. They destroyed the settlement at Zwaanendael, killing all of the settlers. When de Vries learned what had happened, he made peace with the Lenni Lenapes. Later he and the rest on the ship returned to the Netherlands.

*"The friends of the murdered chief incited [encouraged] their friends ... to set about the work of vengeance [revenge]."*
—David Pietersen de Vries, 1632

# Chapter 3:
# New Sweden

After the Dutch left Delaware, settlers from Sweden arrived. In 1637 Swedish businessmen created the New Sweden Company. This trading company formed the colony of New Sweden along the Delaware River. The river provided a path of transportation for merchant ships, and the soil nearby was good for farming.

Swedish colonists arrived on the Delaware shore in 1638.

## Did You Know?

At the time the New Sweden colony began, Sweden's Queen Christina was only 12 years old.

The New Sweden Company purchased land from the Lenni Lenapes in 1638 near the present-day city of Wilmington. They also built Fort Christina, named for Sweden's Queen Christina. Fort Christina became the first settlement of New Sweden. At that time most Swedish citizens did not want to move to America. They had good land at home and didn't want to start over in a strange land. So the government ordered soldiers and other men who had committed minor crimes to move to New Sweden. The Swedish government also persuaded their immigrants from neighboring Finland to move to America. Women and children went to the colony later.

## Farming as a Way of Life

Nearly all of the original colonists in New Sweden had farms and lived peaceful lives. They brought pigs, sheep, and cattle with them to their new land. The colonists built homes and grew corn, peas, beans, wheat, and barley to feed their families.

Along the Delaware River, Swedish colonists grew and harvested crops for food.

## Growth under a New Governor

In 1643 Sweden sent a new governor, Johan Printz, to the colony. The Dutch and English in nearby areas had already made trade agreements with the Native Americans. Printz came up with a new trading plan for the colonists. He realized that New Sweden's colonists would have to travel farther inland to find Native Americans who would trade with them.

DELAWARE

Delaware's Swedish colonists traded with the Lenni Lenapes.

Printz treated the Native Americans respectfully, and his trading plan was successful. New forts and outposts were built along the Delaware River. The colonists planted tobacco to trade and sell. A shipbuilding business opened at Fort Christina.

Printz established the capital of New Sweden at New Gothenburg (near present-day Philadelphia, Pennsylvania). New Sweden grew, but it never had a population larger than a couple hundred people.

## Johan Printz (1592–1663)

Johan Printz studied to be a minister, like his father. However, his family ran out of money before he could finish school. So Printz entered the Swedish Army around the age of 33. He was put in charge of the cavalry—soldiers who rode horses. Printz remained in the army for 20 years.

In 1642 Printz was chosen to be the governor of New Sweden. Printz was energetic and good at getting things done, but his strong personality also created conflict with some of the colonists. Tensions grew, and Printz gave up his rule, returning to Sweden after being governor for 10 years.

# Chapter 4:
# Conflict Over the Land

In the 1650s the Dutch wanted to regain control of the land they had claimed for the Netherlands. They returned to take Delaware back from Sweden. In 1651 Dutch workers built Fort Casimir only about 6 miles south of the Swedish Fort Christina. The location of Fort Casimir meant the Dutch were in control of traffic going up the Delaware River. This made the Swedish colonists angry. Under their new governor, Johan Claesson Rising, New Sweden's residents fought against the Dutch and took control of Fort Casimir. But not for long.

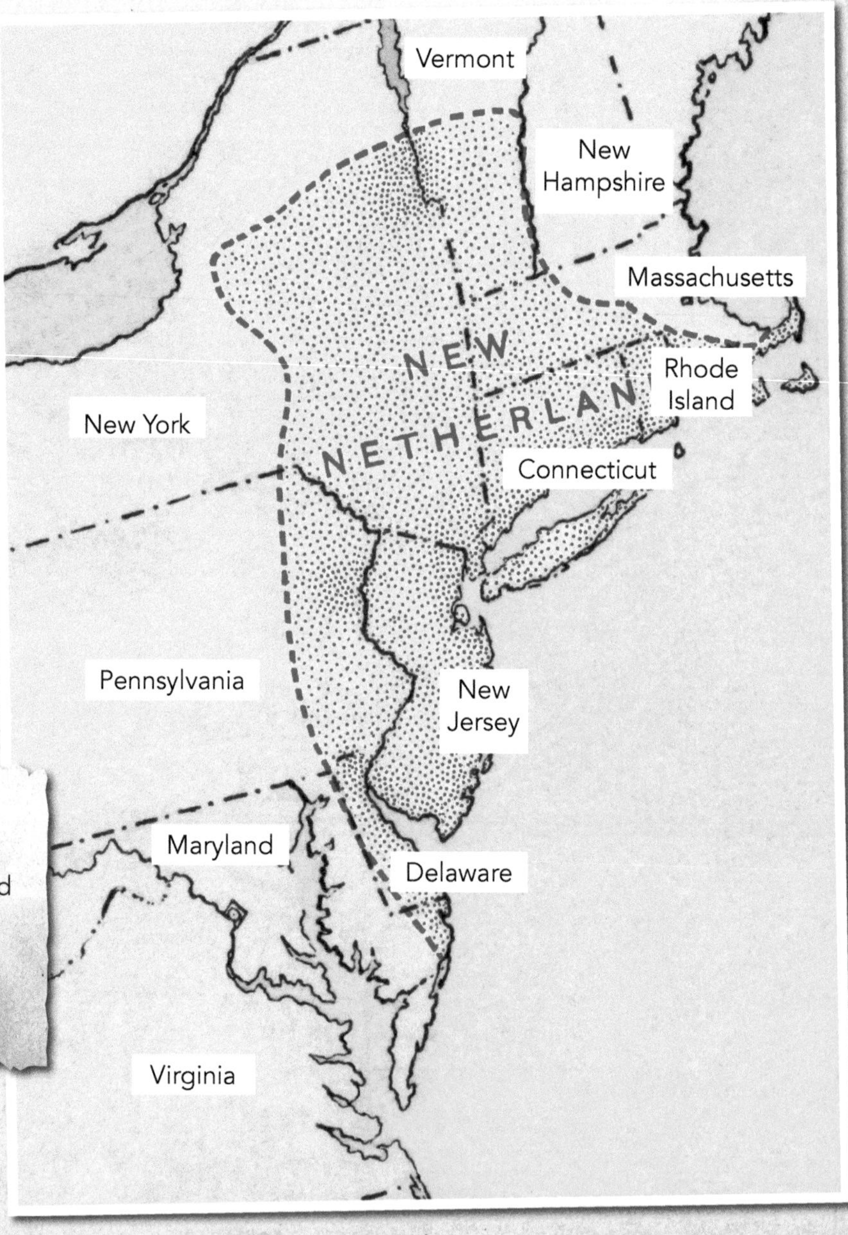

The area of land in America claimed by the Dutch was called New Netherland. Present-day state names are included on the map.

Vermont

New Hampshire

Massachusetts

Rhode Island

New York

NEW NETHERLAND

Connecticut

Pennsylvania

New Jersey

Maryland

Delaware

Virginia

# Critical Thinking with Primary Sources

This map shows how Fort Christina was attacked by the Dutch. Why did the mapmaker draw ships on the water? How did the mapmaker know what size to make Fort Christina on the map? Who probably used this map in 1655?

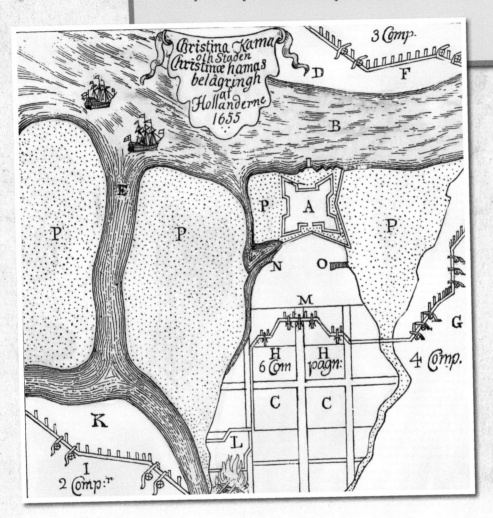

In 1655 the Dutch fought back. Their army took control of Fort Casimir and Fort Christina. The Swedish colonists did not have the military strength to stop the Dutch. But instead of leaving, many Swedish colonists stayed and lived side-by-side with the Dutch colonists. The Dutch made improvements to the area. They built **dikes** and drained swamps so they could use more land for farming. They used the power of windmills to grind grain into flour.

**dike**—a strong wall built to keep water from flooding the land

# England Gains Control

In the mid-1600s King Charles II of England became more and more interested in the American Colonies. Years before, Samuel Argall had claimed the Delaware area for England, but the English never settled the area. England controlled New England, to the north of New Netherland, and Virginia, to the south. Now King Charles II wanted all of the land for England. He didn't care that the Dutch were already there. So the king gave his brother, the Duke of York, the land that belonged to the Netherlands.

Peter Stuyvesant surrendered New Netherland to the English without a fight in 1664.

# Peter Stuyvesant (1592–1672)

Born in the Netherlands around 1592, Peter Stuyvesant spent his early life as a soldier. He then served his country as the governor of several colonies in the New World. He first became the acting governor of Curacao, a Dutch-controlled island in the Caribbean Sea. During a battle for one of the islands, Stuyvesant's right leg was injured. The leg had to be **amputated,** so he wore a wooden leg to help him walk.

In 1647 Stuyvesant became the governor of the Dutch colony of New Netherland. He established a market in New Netherland and worked out agreements with the Native Americans. In 1655 Stuyvesant led the successful takeover of New Sweden. Although he tried to gather troops to fight off the English in 1664, he was advised to surrender instead. Stuyvesant continued to live in New Netherland even after it came under English rule and was renamed New York.

In 1664 the Duke of York sent 450 English soldiers to gain control of the land. The Dutch surrendered because they did not have enough soldiers to fight. The British took over without firing a single shot. They renamed the area New York, including the land along the Delaware River. Present-day Delaware then became part of the New York Colony.

For a while very little changed for the Dutch and Swedish colonists who lived there. Their new rulers allowed them to keep their property, their freedom of religion, and their customs. They continued farming, fishing, and trading.

**amputate**—to cut off someone's arm, leg, or other body part

# Chapter 5:
# Tied to Pennsylvania

Delaware did not remain under the New York Colony's rule. It became part of a new colony. In 1681 Quaker leader William Penn was given a **charter** to start a new colony in America. The Quakers—a religious group that believed in nonviolence and equality for all men and women—were teased and bullied in England. Penn wanted to create a colony where the Quakers could practice their religion in peace. King Charles II named the colony Pennsylvania. Penn named the capital Philadelphia, which is Greek for "brotherly love."

As shown in this engraving, William Penn wanted to live in peaceful friendship with the Lenni Lenapes.

*"I desire to enjoy it [the land] with your love and consent, that we may always live together as neighbors and friends."*

—William Penn to the Lenni Lenape tribe, October 18, 1681

Penn realized quickly that his colony's location, away from Delaware Bay and the Atlantic Ocean, would make trade difficult. Penn asked his friend, the Duke of York, if he could have the land bordering the Delaware River. The Duke of York agreed. This area, known as the "Lower Counties on the Delaware," would later become the state of Delaware.

## Tamanend (1628?–1698?)

Tamanend was a Lenni Lenape chief. He was respected for his wisdom, friendliness, and courtesy to others. Tamanend and other Lenni Lenape chiefs met with William Penn in Philadelphia in 1683. The chiefs agreed to let Penn buy four pieces of land as long as the Lenni Lenapes could still live there too. Tamanend made the mark of a coiled snake for his signature on the agreement to show he approved. Later Tamanend said, "We will live in love with William Penn and his children, as long as the creeks and rivers run, and while the sun, moon, and stars endure."

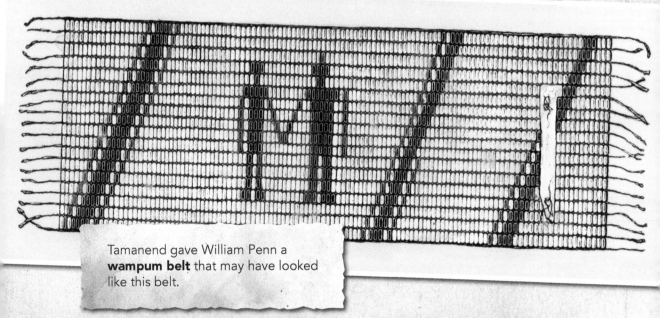

Tamanend gave William Penn a **wampum belt** that may have looked like this belt.

**charter**—an official document granting permission to set up a new colony, organization, or company

**wampum belt**—a belt with shell beads (wampum) used for gifts or for recording stories

## Pennsylvania and the Lower Counties

Penn wanted the three counties in Pennsylvania and the three Lower Counties to have equal power in the Colonial government. He made sure each county was able to send the same number of **representatives** to Philadelphia.

At first the colonists in the Lower Counties were pleased with the government. But later many disagreements developed. The Lower Counties were afraid of being attacked by France or Spain because of their position along the Delaware Bay. They wanted to build forts for protection, but the Quakers refused. The Quakers believed that war, for any reason, was wrong.

Pennsylvania colonists were worried about their location on the Delaware River.

## Did You Know?

Delaware was never a completely separate colony under English rule. Instead it was part of Pennsylvania's two governments. One government was for the "Upper Counties" and the other for the "Lower Counties."

## Differences Grow

In 1685 pirates started attacking English ships and settlements along the Delaware River. Captain Kidd was one of many pirates to bring his ship into the Delaware Bay. It was loaded with treasure stolen from ships on the Indian Ocean. Some colonists from the Lower Counties snuck onto his ship in order to buy silks and other loot. Penn eventually caught the men, and they had to give up the treasures as punishment for dealing with a pirate. But Captain Kidd's crew took small boats to the Delaware shore, where legend claims they hid other treasure.

Other pirates had no interest in trading with colonists. Instead they raided towns and took prisoners. The Lower Counties decided to defend themselves. Without any help from Pennsylvania, they formed a **militia**. Ordinary citizens joined together to fight the pirates. Relations between Pennsylvania and the Lower Counties continued to decline over the next 15 years.

## Move toward Independence

In 1704 Penn allowed the Lower Counties to form their own government in New Castle. Although they still shared a governor with Pennsylvania, the Lower Counties were able to make their own laws. This change brought a lot of independence to the Delaware region.

Legends say Kidd hid treasure on Delaware's shores.

**representative**—someone who is chosen to act or speak for others

**militia**—a group of volunteer citizens who are organized to fight but are not professional soldiers

# Chapter 6:
# Life in the Lower Counties

Between 1700 and 1760, the population in the Lower Counties grew from 3,000 to 35,000 people. Scots-Irish settlers from northern Ireland immigrated because of poor treatment by the British government. Immigrants from Wales came to worship freely. German immigrants moved to the Lower Counties for the good farmland.

## The City of Wilmington

In 1731 Thomas Willing started a town near the Christina River. He designed it in a grid pattern and built homes to sell. He thought his town, called Willingtown, would attract settlers because of its **port**. However, the town did not grow much in the first few years.

Delaware's Colonial capital building is used today as a courthouse.

# Elizabeth Shipley

Elizabeth Shipley was influential in the growth of Willingtown (Wilmington), Delaware. Shipley was a Quaker preacher in Pennsylvania. She had a special dream in the early 1730s. In her dream Shipley saw herself riding to the top of a hill to view a village near several rivers. She believed that God was directing her to move to that village. But she did not know where the village was.

In 1735 Shipley traveled to the Lower Counties. While there, she saw the village of Willingtown for the first time. It was the village in her dream! She convinced her husband William to visit. Her husband saw the great possibilities for trade in Willingtown. He bought land, moved his family there, and started a successful marketplace.

Then in 1735 a rich Quaker merchant named William Shipley decided to move from Ridley, Pennsylvania, to Willingtown. Shipley convinced several other Quaker families to move also. He and his friends built a marketplace where farmers could sell their crops. He also built a dock on the river so that goods could be shipped to other colonies, Europe, and islands in the Caribbean.

Other residents of Willingtown started their own market on land provided by Willing. Willingtown soon grew into a center of trade and shipping and became the largest town in the Lower Counties. In a few years, the name was changed to Wilmington in honor of one of the king's friends.

**port**—a harbor or place where boats and ships can dock or anchor safely

# Farming in Kent and Sussex

Two of the Lower Counties, Kent and Sussex, remained farm country even as towns such as Wilmington grew. Most people in these counties lived on small farms. They raised cows, chickens, and pigs to feed their families. They also grew corn and wheat for their families and to sell at the marketplace.

Tobacco was grown on large farms called plantations. Most of the work on the plantations was done by captured people brought from Africa. The planters did not pay these slaves for their work. The planters and their slaves picked and dried the tobacco, packed it in barrels, and shipped it out of New Castle to other countries. The planters became rich off the tobacco trade and the work of slaves.

In 1750 one out of every 20 people in the Lower Counties was a slave. However, some of the settlers in the Lower Counties, such as the Quakers, thought slavery was wrong. They urged their fellow settlers to free their slaves.

Slaves did most of the work on tobacco plantations in the Lower Counties.

## Critical Thinking with Primary Sources

This painting by John Rubens Smith shows a mill on the Brandywine Creek. What colors did the painter choose to use? How do you think the painter felt about the mills and the colony of Delaware? What important natural features did the artist include in the painting?

# Industries in the Lower Counties

The third of the Lower Counties, New Castle, was known for its towns and industries. The settlers built **mills**, which were powered by the rivers in the area. The flowing water turned a large wooden wheel in the mill. The wheel was connected to gears that turned grinding stones. Grains of wheat were crushed between the grinding stones to become flour. The flour was sold locally or shipped overseas.

Water from the rivers was also used in lumber mills. The water provided power for cutting logs into boards that could be used to build houses and ships. The lumber mills helped the shipbuilding businesses in the area grow. Barrel making also became an important industry in the Lower Counties.

**mill**—a building with machines for turning wood, grain, or other materials into products

## Religious Movement

Along with industries, religious practices gained energy in the Lower Counties in the 1730s and 1740s. During this time a preacher named George Whitefield visited the Lower Counties. He gave lively, emotional sermons on the need to turn away from wrong deeds and follow God. Whitefield convinced Christian people to focus on a personal relationship with God rather than church rituals. This religious movement spread throughout the American Colonies. It was called the Great Awakening.

George Whitefield's sermons drew large crowds during the mid-1700s.

Colonists played a popular lawn bowling game for entertainment.

## Daily Life

In the Lower Counties, every member of a family spent most of the day doing some kind of work. Children helped to cook and clean and care for the farm animals and crops. Most children in the Lower Counties did not attend school. In fact many Lower County residents did not know how to read or write. The Quakers to the north valued education and built schools for their children. But there were no public schools in Colonial Delaware.

## Meals

In the Lower Counties, the biggest meal of the day was breakfast. The lightest meal was eaten in the evening. Stews and soups were cooked in big pots that hung over the fireplace. Colonists drank milk and tea and alcoholic beverages, too, like hard cider and beer.

## Entertainment

Although they worked hard, colonists still found time to have fun. Many families played card games. Children played with toys such as tops, kites, dominoes, and rocking horses. Children also had contests to see who could keep a wooden hoop rolling the longest.

At parties and county fairs, colonists danced and laughed together. Women gathered to sew quilts and clothing. Men played bowling games and held shooting contests. In the winter many families went ice-skating.

# Chapter 7:
# Road to Independence

By 1765 the 13 Colonies were basically governing themselves. But Britain wanted to make more money from the colonies to pay for protecting them. In 1754 France and England fought over land in North America. Native American tribes fought on both sides, and the colonists backed the British. Britain won the French and Indian War in 1763, but the war was expensive. To make money Britain began to tax colonists for tea, paper, and other items. Many colonists were angry. They didn't think they should have to pay taxes because they had no say in Britain's government. Some colonies wanted to be free from Britain and its rules.

Colonists publicly protested the taxes on items such as tea and paper.

## War Begins

In 1774 representatives from each colony met at the Continental Congress to try to settle their complaints with Britain. The Lower Counties sent George Read, Thomas McKean, and Caesar Rodney. But the colonies and Britain could not agree. In 1775 the Revolutionary War began with the Battles of Lexington and Concord in Massachusetts.

The Lower Counties officially split from Pennsylvania in 1776. On June 15 the Lower Counties became an independent state—Delaware—and declared independence from Britain. Delaware's leaders wrote a state constitution later that year.

During the war the Continental Congress met again. At the Second Continental Congress, the colonies voted on whether or not to break free from Britain. To declare independence all 13 Colonies had to agree. When each of the colonies voted for independence, Delaware was the last to vote. Delaware's representatives had differing opinions. McKean wanted independence. Read did not. It was up to Rodney to break the tie for Delaware. He was not there, but he arrived just in time to cast the final vote. Delaware voted for independence. Therefore all the American Colonies declared themselves free of British rule on July 4, 1776.

## Did You Know?

Rodney's famous ride to make the final vote earned him a portrait on the Delaware state quarter, made in 1999.

# Winning Freedom

The colonies were not really free yet. First they had to win the war with Great Britain. The war lasted for eight years but left Delaware mostly untouched. Although naval battles took place in Delaware Bay, the only land battle fought in Delaware was the Battle of Cooch's Bridge in 1777.

As British and German troops marched through Delaware, American troops under William Maxwell met them at Iron Hill, near the town of Newark. Cooch's Bridge crossed a creek at the base of the hill. On September 3, 1777, the sides exchanged gunfire, but the American troops ran out of ammunition. They retreated back across the bridge. About 20 soldiers were killed on each side. No Delaware soldiers fought in the battle, but General Rodney's Delaware militia later fought against the British. The British surrendered after the Battle of Yorktown in Virginia in 1781. After the signing of the Treaty of Paris in 1783, America finally won the war and its independence.

Head of

Lian

## Did You Know?

Some historians believe the Battle of Cooch's Bridge was the first battle into which the American flag was carried.

# Critical Thinking with Primary Sources

This is part of a larger map that shows the movements of the British Army from August through September 1777. It includes the Battle of Cooch's Bridge near Iron Hill. Can you find the note about the battle? Based on the note, which side do you think made this map—the British or the Americans?

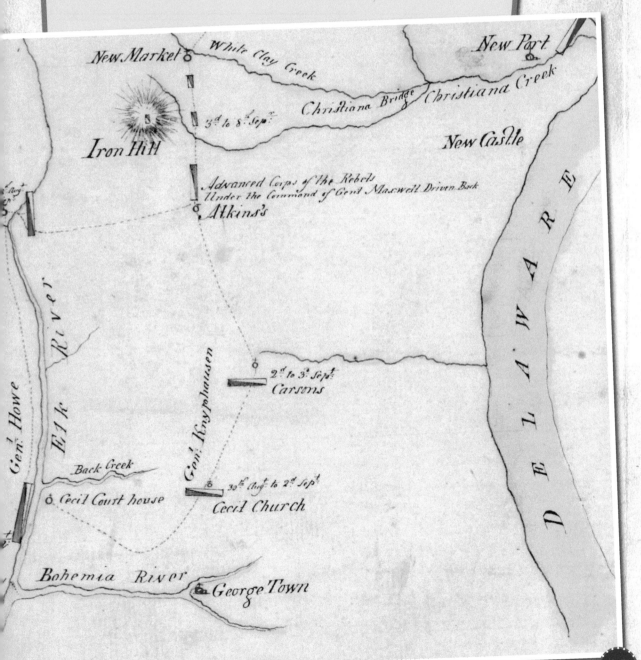

## Becoming a State

After the war representatives from the former colonies created the U.S. Constitution. The Constitution became the basis of a central government for all the states. On December 7, 1787, Delaware became the first state when it **ratified** the U.S. Constitution. Today Delaware's nickname is "the First State."

Delaware became the first state when it approved the U.S. Constitution.

## Caesar Rodney (1728–1784)

Caesar Rodney was born on a farm near Dover on October 7, 1728. He held many offices in government from a young age. From 1774 to 1776, Rodney was a member of the Continental Congress. He became a state hero when Congress was waiting on Delaware's vote to declare independence. Rodney was back home in Delaware, but he got word that his vote was needed. He was sick, but he rode a horse 80 miles through a storm. He arrived in Philadelphia in time to vote for independence from Britain.

During the Revolutionary War, Rodney commanded the Delaware militia. He later served as the governor of Delaware from 1778 to 1781. He died in his home on June 26, 1784, just a year after the United States won its independence from Britain.

**ratify**—to formally approve

# Timeline

**1609** Henry Hudson sails into Delaware Bay and claims the land for the Dutch.

**1610** Samuel Argall names Delaware Bay after Virginia Governor De La Warr.

**1631** The Dutch settle Zwaanendael.

**1632** Captain David Pietersen de Vries discovers Zwaanendael has been destroyed.

**1638** Peter Minuit establishes the New Sweden colony with Swedish and Finnish settlers; Fort Christina is built.

**1643** Johan Printz becomes governor of New Sweden.

**1651** The Dutch build Fort Casimir just south of Fort Christina.

**1655** The Dutch take over New Sweden and add it to their colony of New Netherland.

**1664** The English take over New Netherland and rename it New York; the Delaware area becomes part of the New York Colony.

**1682** The Duke of York gives present-day Delaware to William Penn for part of his Pennsylvania Colony.

**1685** The Lower Counties form their own militia.

**1704** Penn allows the Lower Counties to form a separate legislature; New Castle becomes the Colonial capital of Delaware.

**1731** The village of Willingtown is established.

**1742** The first flour mill is built along the Brandywine River at Wilmington.

**1765** The Stamp Act forces taxes on Delaware and the other American Colonies.

**1774** The Lower Counties send representatives to the First Continental Congress.

**1775** The Revolutionary War begins.

**1776** Delaware (formerly the Lower Counties) declares freedom from England and separates from Pennsylvania.

**1777** The Battle of Cooch's Bridge takes place at Iron Hill near Newark.

**1783** The Revolutionary War ends.

**1787** Delaware becomes the first state when it ratifies the U.S. Constitution.

# Glossary

**amputate** (AM-pyuh-tayt)—to cut off someone's arm, leg, or other body part

**charter** (CHAR-tuhr)—an official document granting permission to set up a new colony, organization, or company

**colony** (KAH-luh-nee)—a place that is settled by people from another country and is controlled by that country

**dike** (DYK)—a strong wall built to keep water from flooding the land

**foliage** (FOH-lee-ij)—leaves

**immigrant** (IM-uh-gruhnt)—someone who comes from one country to live permanently in another country

**indigo** (IN-duh-goh)—a plant that produces a deep-blue dye

**militia** (muh-LISH-uh)—a group of volunteer citizens who are organized to fight but are not professional soldiers

**mill** (MIL)—a building with machines for turning wood, grain, or other materials into products

**natural resource** (NACH-ur-uhl REE-sorss)—a material found in nature that is useful to people

**port** (PORT)—a harbor or place where boats and ships can dock or anchor safely

**ratify** (RAT-uh-fye)—to formally approve

**representative** (rep-ri-ZEN-tuh-tiv)—someone who is chosen to act or speak for others

**smallpox** (SMAWL-poks)—a disease that spreads easily from person to person, causing chills, fever, and pimples that scar

**tolerance** (TOL-ur-uhnss)—the acceptance of people's beliefs or actions that differ from one's own beliefs or actions

**wampum belt** (WAHM-puhm BELT)—a belt with shell beads (wampum) used for gifts or for recording stories

**wigwam** (WIG-whahm)—a hut made of poles covered with bark, leaves, or animal skins

# Critical Thinking Using the Common Core

1. What happened to the first Dutch settlement in Delaware? (Key Ideas and Details)
2. Which paragraphs help you understand what life was like in Colonial times? Where did you look to find these paragraphs? (Craft and Structure)
3. What might have happened if Caesar Rodney didn't make it to Philadelphia to vote for independence? What would it mean if he voted against independence? (Integration of Knowledge and Ideas)

# Read More

**Cunningham, Kevin**. *The Delaware Colony*. New York: Children's Press, 2012.

**Lee, David**. *The Colony of Delaware*. New York: PowerKids Press, 2016.

**Micklos, John Jr.** *The Making of the United States from Thirteen Colonies through Primary Sources*. Berkeley Heights, N.J.: Enslow Publishers, 2013.

**Pratt, Mary K**. *A Timeline History of the Thirteen Colonies*. Minneapolis, Minn.: Lerner Publications, 2014.

# Internet Sites

FactHound offers a safe, fun way to find Internet sites related to this book. All of the sites on FactHound have been researched by our staff.
Here's all you do:
Visit *www.facthound.com*
Type in this code: 9781515722397

Super-cool stuff!

Check out projects, games and lots more at
**www.capstonekids.com**

## Source Notes

Page 6, line 18 quote: John de Laet. "Extracts from the New World or A Description of the West Indies by John de Laet." *Collections of the New-York Historical Society*. 2nd ser., Vol. 1. New York: H. Ludwig, 1841, p. 290.

Page 8, callout quote: Peter Lindstrom. *Geographia Americae*. New York: Arno Press, 1925, p. 175.

Page 17, callout quote: David Pietersen de Vries. *Voyages from Holland to America, A.D. 1632 to 1644*. Translated by Henry C. Murphy. New York: James Lenox, 1853, p. 34.

Page 26, callout quote: William Penn. "William Penn to the Kings of the Indians in Pennsylvania, October 18, 1681." From the Penn Family Papers at the Historical Society of Pennsylvania: Philadelphia. Accessed December 9, 2015. http://digitalhistory.hsp.org/pafrm/doc/william-penn-kings-indians-pennsylvania-october-18-1681.

Page 27, biography box, line 7: "William Penn's Treaty with the Indians at Shackamaxon." Penn Treaty Museum. Accessed April 18, 2016. http://www.penntreatymuseum.org/treaty.php.

## Regions of the 13 Colonies

| Northern Colonies | Middle Colonies | Southern Colonies |
|---|---|---|
| Connecticut, Massachusetts, New Hampshire, Rhode Island | Delaware, New Jersey, New York, Pennsylvania | Georgia, Maryland, North Carolina, South Carolina, Virginia |
| land more suitable for hunting than farming; trees cut down for lumber; trapped wild animals for their meat and fur; fished in rivers, lakes, and ocean | the "Breadbasket" colonies—rich farmland, perfect for growing wheat, corn, rye, and other grains | soil better for growing tobacco, rice, and indigo; crops grown on huge farms called plantations; landowners depended heavily on servants and slaves to work in the fields |

# Select Bibliography

"Extracts from the New World or A Description of the West Indies by John de Laet." *Collections of the New-York Historical Society*. 2nd ser., Vol. 1. New York: H. Ludwig, 1841.

Gray, Edward G. *Colonial America: A History in Documents*. New York: Oxford University Press, 2003.

Hossell, Karen. *Delaware: 1638–1776*. Washington, D.C.: National Geographic Society, 2006.

Lindstrom, Peter. *Geographia Americae*. New York: Arno Press, 1925, p. 175.

Lukes, Bonnie L. *Colonial America*. San Diego: Lucent Books, 2000.

Penn, William. "William Penn to the Kings of the Indians in Pennsylvania, October 18, 1681." From the Penn Family Papers at the Historical Society of Pennsylvania: Philadelphia. Accessed December 9, 2015. http://digitalhistory.hsp.org/pafrm/doc/william-penn-kings-indians-pennsylvania-october-18-1681.

Taylor, Alan. *American Colonies*. New York: Viking, 2001.

Vries, David Pietersen de. *Voyages from Holland to America, A.D. 1632 to 1644*. Translated by Henry C. Murphy. New York: James Lenox, 1853.

"William Penn's Treaty with the Indians at Shackamaxon." Penn Treaty Museum. Accessed April 18, 2016. http://www.penntreatymuseum.org/treaty.php.

# Index